DEMOCRACY BLINDFOLDED:
THE CASE FOR A FREEDOM OF INFORMATION
ACT IN IRELAND

UNDERCURRENTS

Published titles in the series

Facing the Unemployment Crisis in Ireland by Kieran Kennedy
Divorce in Ireland: Who Should Bear the Cost? by Peter Ward
Crime and Crisis in Ireland: Justice by Illusion? by Caroline Fennell
The Hidden Tradition: Feminism, Women and Nationalism in Ireland
by Carol Coulter
Managing the EU Structural Funds by Alan Matthews
*Diverse Communities: The Evolution of Lesbian and Gay Politics in
Ireland* by Kieran Rose

Forthcoming titles will include

Susan Ryan Sheridan on new reproductive technologies
Jim MacLaughlin on new-wave emigration

UNDERCURRENTS Series Editor Fintan O'Toole

Democracy Blindfolded: The Case for a Freedom of Information Act in Ireland

PATRICK SMYTH AND RONAN BRADY

CORK UNIVERSITY PRESS

First published in 1994 by
Cork University Press
University College
Cork
Ireland

British Library Cataloguing in Publication Data

A CIP catalogue record for this book is available from the British Library

ISBN 1 85918 040 X

Typeset in Ireland by Seton Music Graphics Ltd, Bantry, Co. Cork
Printed in Ireland by ColourBooks, Baldoyle, Co. Dublin

'There is not a crime, there is not a dodge, there is not a trick, there is not a swindle, there is not a vice which does not live by secrecy. Get these things out into the open, describe them, attack them, ridicule them in the press, and sooner or later public opinion will sweep them away. Publicity may not be the only thing that is needed, but it is the one thing without which all other agencies will fail.'

(Joseph Pulitzer)

'I think that if the questions that were asked in the Dáil were answered in the way they are answered here, there would be no necessity for this inquiry and an awful lot of money and time would have been saved.'

(Mr Justice Liam Hamilton at the Beef Industry Tribunal, January 1992)

CONTENTS

1. Introduction   1

2. Secrecy, Bureaucracy and the Beef Tribunal   7

3. The International Experience   12

4. Will it Work under our System?   27

5. Letting in the Light?   37

Notes and References   44

Appendices   47

1. Introduction

When Charles Haughey introduced his updated Official Secrets Act in 1962 as Minister for Justice he was unapologetic about its scope: 'We are dealing with the disclosure of official information, whether it is of a serious or of a comparatively trivial importance . . . In other words if a document is stamped or marked officially as secret and confidential, then that comes within the definition of official information which may not be disclosed without proper authority . . . Surely a minister or government is entitled to decide whether a thing is secret or confidential and mark it as such?'

Surely? The answer to that question in many countries today is 'no'. The answer in two human rights conventions to which Ireland is party is also 'no'. Others have decided that the presumption of secrecy – the idea that all is secret unless specifically deemed not to be so – is bad for government and democracy. It shields the incompetent and the crooked and denies the public access to the workings of democracy. Information is power, and so democracy means sharing information.

The right of the public to access to information held by the state, whether personal files on the individual citizen, or access to the policy process, is now very clearly established in international law and is the growing practice in western democracies. The Irish system of almost obsessive secrecy is another of the legacies of the British administrative tradition whose philosophy is best summed up in the words of Sir Humphrey Appleby in *Yes Minister*: 'Open government is a contradiction in terms. You can have openness, or you can have government'. It is a view not shared by all British politicians, however. Lord Egremont, Harold Macmillan's private secretary, considered all spying and secrets a waste of time and money. 'Much better,' he said, 'if the Russians saw the cabinet minutes twice a week. Prevent all that fucking dangerous guess-work'. For Russians read 'public'.

Are the powers of the state in Ireland really proportionate to the problems that public access to most state papers would pose? Is it really necessary to classify everything in order to protect a small number of documents that may, arguably, need to be secret in the national interest or for the sake of privacy? Or is the truth really that it suits both government and administration to cloak their dealings in a veil of secrecy?

Sometimes the slogan 'Freedom of Information' can sound like a battle-cry in the unending war between journalists and politicians; a debate between sections of the élite which is of little relevance to the lives of ordinary voters. But it is a vital issue for ordinary citizens and the lack of it has diminished the standing of both journalists and politicians in their eyes. Voters are sick to death with the cute-hoorism of the Irish political process and are demanding the right to make informed choices at the ballot box. For that to happen, the Official Secrets Act must go and light must be shed on the dark recesses of government.

Our pamphlet is designed as a contribution to a debate which has already begun. The current Programme for Government undertakes to consider the introduction of a Freedom of Information Bill and Eithne Fitzgerald, junior minister at the Office of the Tánaiste, is now taking submissions on the subject. Her general proposals go a long way to meeting the case proposed in this pamphlet. But they have yet to be fleshed out in detail or to face the inevitably hostile reaction of ministers and public servants used to the old ways.

Today, freedom of information is seen as a vital part of democracy in other European countries. Powerful people in this country can not fend it off for ever.

MORE WHITEHALL THAN WHITEHALL ITSELF

Although based upon a British model, Irish law embodies a distinctly more restrictive conception of secrecy than its colonial predecessor.

In March 1962, Justice Minister Charles Haughey claimed to be merely 'consolidating' previous British legislation,[1] modernizing it and making it appropriate to Irish conditions, when he introduced the Official Secrets Bill.[2] In fact, he overrode important principles of human rights and substituted ministerial discretion for the traditional role of the courts in deciding what is, and what is not to be secret.

The key passages of this Act make it clear that the primary duty of a civil servant is to suppress information, disclosure being the exception rather than the rule:

> A person shall not communicate any official information to any other person unless he is duly authorized to do so or does so in the course of and in accordance with his duties as the holder of a public office or when it is his duty in the interest of the State to communicate it.[3]

Charles Haughey's major innovation was to give government ministers the final say on whether information is secret. Previously, those charged under official secrets legislation could challenge the state's case on the basis that the leaked information was not really secret. In the present act, the term 'official information' covers any 'sketch, plan, model, article, note, document, or information which is secret or confidential or is expressed to be either and which is or has been in the possession, custody or control of a holder of public office'. Should any minister or state authority classify a document as 'secret', then it is illegal to divulge it. Haughey took the 'top secret' stamp out of the hands of the courts and placed it in the hands of politicians, who shun public scrutiny, and in those of the bureaucracy itself. Not only is it illegal for public officials to impart any information whatsoever if it has a 'confidential' tag, it is also forbidden to obtain official information if the person doing so has 'reasonable grounds' for believing that the information has been labelled 'secret'. Journalists as well as civil servants come within this net of the secrecy law.

In his introduction, Haughey grouped together as reasons for the new security law international espionage, collaboration with the IRA, and a case two years previously where a printer divulged the contents of exam papers to students. His suggestion was that any breach of secrecy was a major one – leaks to the KGB, the IRA and a forged birth certificate were somehow of a par. In the atmosphere of the time, one of intense anti-communism after the Cuban missile crisis, this was extremely effective. Civil servants had been warned.

Haughey's attempt to drag in the exam scandal raised the hackles of a number of opposition speakers. 'Could the school-children to whom the printer sold his information be prosecuted under the Bill?' asked John Dillon and Patrick McGilligan in the Dáil. After all, they would have obtained confidential information, knowing it was confidential. The Minister remained silent on this point. These exchanges prompted Gerard Sweetman of Fine Gael to remark that he had just thrown out a seven-year-old memo regarding a budget he had drawn up during a previous coalition government. The memo was marked 'secret' because it was secret at the time. But, seven years after the budget was delivered, could it still be considered confidential? It was 'still a secret document', replied Haughey.[4]

The laughter provoked by these contradictions evaporated when Sections 9 and 10 of the Official Secrets Act, dealing with state security, came up for discussion. The crucial element of these sections dispenses with the presumption of innocence, one of the most fundamental civil rights. If it can be proved that a person charged under the Act visited the address of a foreign agent or an IRA member, then he will 'unless he proves to the contrary, be deemed to have been in communication' with that person. Worse still, simply having the address of an IRA member or a spy in one's notebook is enough to be found guilty on this score. And, if push comes to shove, any address 'reasonably suspected' of belonging to a foreign agent or a member of a banned organization, will be sufficient to prove that one has broken the Official Secrets Act.

With regard to the Defence Forces and the Gárdai, it is an offence to possess any information at all without the permission of the relevant Minister. But – just in case the point is not made clear enough – during official secrets trials involving state security, if the prosecution alleges that a matter endangers the safety of the state, the hearings must be held in camera.

Certainly there will be secrets cases which, it can be argued, should be held behind closed doors. But the Irish Official Secrets Act allows the prosecution, rather than the judge, to decide that matter. A person 'reasonably suspected' of such an offence, or of 'being about to' do so, may be arrested without a warrant. The courts can be bypassed if gárdai wish to search premises. A Gárda chief superintendent may issue a search warrant under Section 9. Such an officer may also authorize a Gárda inspector to demand information on the alleged offence. Refusal to comply with such a demand means the suspect loses the right to silence and that the court is entitled to draw an inference from such behaviour.

In the Dáil M.J. O'Higgins warned that these provisions 'can be used in a very vicious way', adding that 'If a person comes in under Section 9, he has had it.' Speaking from the government benches, Major Vivion de Valera questioned the legislation, suggesting that instead of furthering 'the interests of the state', it was designed for 'the convenience of the administration'. James Tully of Labour objected to sections of the Bill which 'embodied the principles underlying the Offences Against the State Act'. To adopt these in 'ordinary legislation' was a 'bad precedent'.

Prosecutions under the Official Secrets Act – usually held in camera – are rare. In 1987 the *Irish Independent* was successfully prosecuted and fined for publishing a police identikit photo despite the fact that the picture had been widely circulated and had previously been published. In 1988 the Act was used against a republican who was listening in to Gárda communications in Harcourt Street. Although rarely used, the act supports a climate of secrecy in the civil service that is all pervasive. It has been reinforced by a Supreme Court decision copperfastening cabinet confidentiality. The case emerged from the Beef Tribunal when the Attorney General challenged the right of tribunal chairperson, Mr Justice Liam Hamilton, to question a cabinet minister about cabinet discussions.

It was argued that the constitutional provision for the cabinet to 'act as a collective authority' and to be 'collectively responsible' for government business meant that ministers could not divulge what went on behind cabinet doors. In the High Court, Mr Justice Rory O'Hanlon agreed with Mr Justice Hamilton's right to question the minister on the grounds of public interest. But this was overturned by the Supreme Court. The Chief Justice, Mr Justice Finlay, delivered the majority verdict that collective responsibility 'involves, as a necessity, the non-disclosure of dissenting voices'.[5] His rationale, like that of those who drafted the Official Secrets Act, was that reading the Constitution in this way made it a more 'effective instrument for the ordering of society and the governing of the nation'. In other words, good government requires secrecy. The decision was not, however, unanimous. Mr Justice Niall McCarthy eloquently argued the opposite case, pointing out that if those who framed the Constitution meant to ban all mention of cabinet disagreements, they could well have done so. The fact that they did not impose such an oath of silence on cabinet ministers argued for Mr Justice Hamilton's rather than the Attorney General's case. Nor does the decision restrict in any way the Dáil's right to pass freedom of information legislation that deals with government outside the cabinet room.

2. SECRECY, BUREAUCRACY AND THE BEEF TRIBUNAL

No more powerful case can be made for a freedom of information act than the extraordinary sequence of events surrounding the Beef Tribunal – the largest investigation into governmental decision-making and administrative practice since the formation of the state. The cost of the tribunal is unlikely to be less than £35 million, while the shadow cast over the reputation of Irish beef producers will probably add to the bill in the long run. In addition, there will be costs to the state for export-credit insurance which is still subject to litigation.

Under the Westminster system, on which the Dáil procedure is based, information which a government choses not to publicize is mainly divulged through parliamentary questions. In theory, an individual TD is entitled to cross-question a minister and each exchange is recorded in the official account of parliamentary proceedings, so there is no wriggling out of a direct undertaking. The trouble is that ministers find it quite easy, under this system, to avoid direct undertakings and to be so economical with the truth that it starves to death. The introduction of a freedom of information regime both legislatively and in terms of Dáil procedure could begin to redress the balance in favour of the public.

The debacle which led to the Beef Industry Tribunal stemmed from the failure of current Dáil procedures to get at the truth – a view shared by Mr Justice Liam Hamilton, chair of the Beef Tribunal. During the testimony of a Department of Agriculture official in January 1992, he stated: 'I think that if the questions that were asked in the Dáil were answered in the way they are answered here, there would be no necessity for this inquiry and an awful lot of money and time would have been saved.'[6]

The crux of this argument is that parliamentary and civil service procedures allow ministers to evade TDs' questions. In furnishing their ministers with answers to parliamentary questions, departmental officials are trained to respond only to the exact question asked by the TD and to deliver not a sliver of additional information. If the information on which the TD bases the original question is too sketchy and the question too general, it will receive a bland, general response. To find something out, a TD must specify exactly what is being sought. That usually means that the TD must know the answer to the question before asking it.

This point emerges clearly as we follow the Beef Tribunal testimony of Mr Donal Russell, the Department of Agriculture official mentioned above. Asked if he saw any difficulty in furnishing the answer to a Dáil question on irregularities, Russell stated that 'It would depend on how the question was put'. Mr Justice Hamilton then asked: 'I think it's true to say and it applies to all administrations, all ministers, all parties that when dealing with, . . . parliamentary questions, it's the policy to give the minimum of information, would that be so?'

There followed a very interesting exchange:

> Russell: 'No, that's not correct, it's the policy to answer the question which is asked.'
> Mr Justice Hamilton: 'And no further?'.
> Russell: 'Yes, that's correct.'
> Mr Justice Hamilton: 'So, if a person asking a question . . . hadn't the full information at his or her disposal, and maybe asked an incomplete or an incorrect question, it's the policy to only answer the question and not to give information that might be helpful . . . in clarifying the position?'
> Russell: 'Well, there is no rule of thumb on this as such but one has to look at a question that's asked and give the information in direct answer to that question but not to offer information.'
> Mr Justice Hamilton: 'Not to offer information.'

Such procedures do not spring from the free, unfettered minds of civil servants. Their source lies in the constant struggle of government ministers to remain one step ahead of the parliament that supervises their work and the natural inclination of the civil servant not to fall foul of his or her boss. But the secrecy and the evasion which are created in this process, erode the power of the individual TD and devalue the parliament.

However unsatisfactory the bureaucratic labyrinth may be, this dissatisfaction is compounded by the stifling effect of parliamentary procedure on the TD's right to question ministers. In theory, Dáil debate is protected by the Ceann Comhairle. In practice, however, interventions by the Ceann Comhairle may have the opposite effect.

Until last May, deputies might seek to raise a matter which had been widely discussed in the public domain. But, if there was any likelihood of a legal case concerning the matter, it was ruled out of order by the chair of the Dáil on the grounds that it was *sub judice*. TDs could point to the fact that the issue had been discussed in the newspapers and on television, but these points were irrelevant to the Ceann Comhairle. The constitutional separation of powers whereby parliaments are not subject to the courts was simply abandoned.[7]

Some of the issues covered by this blanket ban would astound the casual observer. Deputies were prevented from hearing government answers on allegations of planning malpractice in Dublin, on drug dealing in Dublin's Thomas Street, on the Greencore affair and on many other subjects, despite the fact that these matters were openly discussed outside the Dáil. Under the reformed standing orders, agreed on 8 April, 1993, members were allowed to raise matters 'even where court proceedings have been initiated'. But the Ceann Comhairle continues to obstruct TDs by disallowing questions on other equally elastic grounds. Two of the most common of these are that the minister has 'no official responsibility' for the matter or, that it is 'hypothetical'. These categories have been stretched to cover almost anything.

In March 1994, Proinsias De Rossa of Democratic Left sought to ask the Taoiseach 'if he has received any indications directly or indirectly that the IRA intends to call a temporary ceasefire; and if he will make a statement on the matter'.[8] Ceann Comhairle, Seán Treacy, disallowed the question on the breathtaking grounds that Albert Reynolds 'has no official responsibility to the Dáil on this matter'.

Aside from absolving the government of responsibility for peace moves in the North, the Ceann Comhairle's rulings also protect the government from questions about semi-state bodies. A question from the same deputy about a meeting between the Taoiseach and the chair of a British telecommunications company interested in Telecom Éireann was also disallowed for the same reason.[9]

Rulings by the present Ceann Comhairle, Seán Treacy, in which he rejects questions because they are 'hypothetical' raise some serious constitutional questions about the relationship between executive and legislature, as well as ruling out of discussion all questions about future events. One questioner sought 'To ask the Taoiseach his priorities for [a] special meeting of the European Council'[10] but Treacy rejected it on the grounds that it was 'hypothetical'.

Clearly, if a minister's objectives at a future meeting are hypothetical, then any future event is hypothetical and is therefore out of bounds. It should be a matter for the executive to argue whether a matter is hypothetical or not, and for the legislature to agree, or not.

The Beef Tribunal also provides us with another example of the Ceann Comhairle's restrictions. In May 1989, newspaper articles began to appear alleging that much less beef had actually been exported to Iraq than the government's export-credit insurance figures suggested. The large gap between the two sets of figures led to questions about major fraud and these were widely discussed in the newspapers and on the airwaves. It later emerged that a considerable amount of beef from Northern Ireland had been passed off as beef from the Irish Republic for the purposes of receiving export-credit insurance.

The Progressive Democrat TD, Pat O'Malley, sought information about this from Ray Burke, then Minister for Industry and Commerce. He submitted a parliamentary question asking for information 'which would explain the major discrepancy between the beef export figures to Iraq for the two years 1987 and 1988 and the export-credit insurance provided for these exports in the same period'.

On May 23rd 1989, the Ceann Comhairle wrote to O'Malley informing him that he 'had to disallow' the above question, on the grounds that it was 'a repeat' of questions previously asked. The Ceann Comhairle continued: 'The question will now read: 'To ask the Minister for Industry and Commerce when he expects the investigations into the major discrepancy between the beef export figures to Iraq for the two years 1987 and 1988 and the export-credit insurance provided for these exports in the same period will be completed; and if he will make a statement on the matter.'[11]

The portion of O'Malley's question which actually sought a clear explanation to the Dáil about the discrepancy was simply chopped off, leaving the minister free to report only on the state of the departmental investigation into the matter. Consequently, Ray Burke provided Pat O'Malley with a written answer informing him that the investigation was being carried out, that it was 'complex', that it was 'receiving priority attention' and that it was 'essential' that the investigation 'be thorough and comprehensive'.

In other words, the answer told him nothing at all about the content of the investigation. As the backbone of the question had already been filleted out, the Minister was perfectly free to do this. But the Ceann Comhairle did allow O'Malley to ask the Minister when the inquiry might finish. The Minister for Industry and Commerce failed even to answer this – on account of its 'complex nature', its 'priority' and the requirement of thoroughness, he concluded, 'I am not in a position to indicate when the investigation will be completed.'[12]

There can be little argument that, by blunting the individual TD's right to find out information, the Dáil rules and the civil service procedures damage the quality of our democracy.

There has recently been much learned discussion of the 'ineffectiveness' of the Dáil,[13] the 'limited' and 'parochial' concerns of TDs who ignore their legislative functions for parish pump issues,[14] and the clientelism of TDs is widely condemned. At the heart of most of the critical literature is the view that the present party system turns the TD into an automaton.

There may well be considerable truth in that, but as the TD is effectively prevented from challenging the government, and as rulings of the Ceann Comhairle stand as a sentry – preventing the release of even the most trivial information – the deputy's contribution is further devalued. The adoption of a freedom of information act, in effect an Irish glasnost, would enhance the power of the individual representative and reduce that of the whips.

For journalists and historians, such a development has obvious benefits, but these are far outweighed by the benefits to TDs from such legislation. Ours is essentially a parliamentary system. The TD is the link between the ordinary voter and the state. Preventing him or her from getting at the truth slaps the general public in the face. Such limits on the power of our parliamentarians disable our democracy.

3. THE INTERNATIONAL EXPERIENCE

It is important to understand that Irish and British records on official secrecy are increasingly out of line with international practice and law. Democracies like the US and Australia, among others, have introduced elaborate and extensive freedom of information legislation over the last 20 years. In Australia about 25,000 people a year apply for access to documents held by the state; in the US that figure is now 250,000 – access has become part of the political culture.

The US Freedom of Information Act has been crucial in unearthing a huge range of scandals and abuses of power, from the stranger excesses of J. Edgar Hoover to the covert operations of Oliver North. Recently it has exposed war-time experiments on mental patients, disinformation about the invasion of Panama, the assurances given by Ambassador Glaspie to Saddam Hussein that the US regarded Iraq's dispute with Kuwait as an essentially private matter, and numerous scandals over election funding on Capitol Hill.

The US learnt its lessons from the debacle of the Vietnam War and the ignominy of Nixon and Watergate. In a classic injunction to government at the end of the Pentagon Papers case, Justice Stewart summed up brilliantly a philosophy for the new age of freedom of information:

> The very first principle [of a wise security system would be] an insistence on avoiding secrecy for its own sake. For when everything is classified, nothing is classified, and the system becomes one to be disregarded by the cynical or careless, and to be manipulated by those intent on self-protection or self-promotion. I should suppose, in short, that the hallmark of a truly effective internal security system would be the maximum possible disclosure, recognising that secrecy can best be preserved only when credibility is truly maintained.[15]

The Swedes, to whom we shall return, have a tradition of openness that goes back to the Freedom of the Press Act of 1766 which is incorporated into their constitution. Their constitution also recognizes the importance of protecting both the source of information and the journalist who publishes it.

Crucially, too, the concept of access to information is embodied in international conventions to which Ireland is party. The Universal Declaration of Human Rights (1948) specifies in Article 19 that:

> Everyone has the right to freedom of opinion and expression: this right includes freedom to hold opinions without interference and to seek, receive and impart information and ideas through any media and regardless of frontiers.

The European Convention on Human Rights (1950), to which Ireland is also a signatory, provides guarantees in Article 10 of the right to freedom of expression –

> this right shall include freedom to hold opinions and to receive and impart information and ideas with out interference by public authority, and regardless of frontiers.

While popular perceptions of Article 19 tend to associate it with the right to free speech, both conventions draw the distinction between the rights to receive and to impart information. For a democracy to function properly, it is argued, the citizen must be able to give informed consent. That is impossible with a regime of secrecy, and so the right to seek information is just as important – some would say more important – than the right to free speech. Even though Article 10 is somewhat less explicit than Article 19 about the right to receive information, and does not specifically guarantee access to official documents, the European Court of Human Rights in an important ruling in 1976[16] insisted on the importance of freedom of information which it said is one of the essential foundations for the progress of democratic society and for the development of the human being.

In 1981 the Committee of Ministers of the Council of Europe adopted a recommendation bringing to the attention of the governments of the member states the desirability of recognizing the right of access to information held by the state. The Committee also considered amending Article 10 of the European Convention on Human Rights, to provide the right more explicitly, but decided not to do so as the Court of Human Rights had, it was felt, made sufficiently clear the right was already implicit in the article.

The following year the Committee adopted a 'Solemn Declaration on the Freedom of Expression and Information' (*see* Appendix 1), effectively a Media Charter. In it, ministers promised to foster free access to information. The Irish government is a signatory to both the Convention on Human Rights, which is enforceable through the European Court of Human Rights, and to both declarations. Until now it has completely failed to act upon either in relation to official secrecy.

Case law in the European Court of Human Rights goes further. The court has recognized the right of the state to restrict freedom of expression and information only in a number of specific areas:

- The protection of the public interest (national security, territorial integrity, public safety, prevention of disorder or crime, protection of health or morals);
- The protection of other individual rights (the protection of reputation or the rights of others, or the prevention of disclosure of information received in confidence);
- Restrictions necessary to maintain the authority and impartiality of the judiciary.[17]

Most importantly, however, the Court holds that in order to be admissible, any restriction must be prescribed by law and necessary 'in a democratic society'. In other words the Court insists on a presumption of openness as being essential to the workings of a democracy. And while the Court will grant states a 'margin of appreciation' – effectively a judicial benefit of the doubt – it insists that 'the necessity for restricting them [the rights under Article 10] must be convincingly established'.[18]

In another ruling in 1993 (Goodwin *v* UK) that will have important consequences for journalists in Ireland, the Commission of Human Rights, which hears preliminary applications to the Court and rules on their admissibility, found against the British House of

Lords which had upheld a fine on a journalist who refused to reveal his sources to a court. The Commission accepted the argument that the protection of journalists' sources, or what is known as journalistic privilege, is an important corollary of the freedoms enshrined in Article 10. Lawyers believe the Court will endorse the Commission's view.

In Lingens v Austria[19] the Court ruled that:

> Penalties against the press for publishing information and opinions concerning matters of public interest are intolerable except in the narrowest of circumstances owing to their likelihood of deterring journalists from contributing to the public discussion of issues affecting the life of the community.

In Ireland the courts have refused to recognize the concept of privilege and a number of journalists still face potential prosecution for failing to reveal sources to the Beef Tribunal. In its 1992 preliminary report on contempt of court, the Law Reform Commission also rejected any reform of the law in this matter.

Not content with making official documents available to the public and protecting journalistic privilege, the US has gone further and in 1978 also recognized explicitly that those who leaked material of public interest to the press should be legally protected. The Civil Service Reform Act – known as the Whistleblower's Act – protects civil servants from legal action and demotion if they disclose any evidence of wrongdoing or malpractice. The act mirrors law in Sweden, Norway, France, and elsewhere.

The Irish courts and state refuse to recognize that the free flow of information is crucial to the functioning of a democracy, and that the press plays an important role in that process. The courts in the Republic have never sought, as those in the US have done with great liberality, to interpret the constitutional guarantee of freedom of the press (Article 40.6.1) in anything except the most narrow way. Nor has the legislature done anything to ease the pressure on the media from extremely restrictive libel and contempt laws.

Yet obstacles to the free flow of information – whether they be in the form of official secrets acts, sanctions against whistleblowers or curbs on journalists' ability to get at information – increasingly fly in the face of mainstream international practice and the international human rights obligations of the state.

Even within the administration of the European Union, Ireland finds itself seriously out of step. Concerned at the increasing alienation of the public throughout the Union manifested by the French and Danish votes on Maastricht, the Council of Foreign Ministers and the Commission agreed in December 1993 to a new code of conduct on access to EU documents. That code institutionalizes a presumption of openness. One commissioner has even claimed, somewhat overstating the case, that 99 per cent of Commission documents are available for scrutiny. Much work still has to be done in the Commission – notably in providing accessible indexing or registering of archives so that researchers can find out what is available – but back in Dublin we are not even in the same ball game.

The European Union widened access to information on the environment on 31 December, 1992. Directive 90/313/EEC compels local, regional and national government bodies in member states to provide environmental information.[20] Unfortunately, its effectiveness is reduced by the wide escape-hatches member states are entitled to use if they don't want to come clean. Among other things, the list of matters which may be exempted from the openness ruling includes issues which are *sub judice* or even 'under enquiry', matters affecting commercial confidentiality, and any information voluntarily provided by a third party.

Someone denied information has the right to a 'judicial or administrative review' of the denial in accordance with the relevant legislative system. But the directive does not clarify the legal basis for such a review to take place. The authors of the directive might have stated that the exemptions could be overridden if the public interest was endangered, but they did not. Instead, they chose to give the member states the maximum opportunity to restrict the effects of the directive.

The Minister for the Environment, Michael Smith, availed very fully of this right when he drafted the regulations which bring the directive into effect in this country. In fact, he provided a gaping exemption whereby a public authority *must* refuse to give information if it relates to 'personal information held in relation to an individual who has not given his consent to the disclosure'. By not allowing any discretion at all on this matter, the minister has left us with a dangerously wide gap in the law which may go much further than simply protecting what is generally seen as personal information.

The minister's regulation virtually invites litigation in cases where, for example, contractors working for public bodies might seek to prevent disclosure of information concerning their practices on the grounds that this is 'personal'. On the question of 'judicial or administrative review', Mr Smith's regulations are totally silent. A set of guidelines accompanying the regulations notes that they set up no new review structures and that 'normal administrative and judicial remedies' will apply if information is refused. A disappointed applicant may ask the authority to reconsider its decision or, in certain cases, invoke the Ombudsman. Finally, the inquirer may turn to the courts.

There is some substance to Directive 90/313 – it will make environmental information more available than before. Guidelines on such matters as factory emissions impose clear responsibilities on companies. The directive will add to the general pressure for openness. But what is notable about this measure is that, when translated into the Irish legal/administrative system, the 'maybe nots' tend to become 'must nots'. Freedom of information Euro-style has to be rather bland so as to get the approval of the various governments. Then it has to be made blander still to fit in with our legal and administrative norms. Finally it has to be enforced – the EU is now demanding an explanation from the government as to why a significant number of councils have failed to respond to a Greenpeace survey of factory emissions.

BRITAIN'S EXPERIENCE

In Britain, the culture of secrecy, although very much still a force, has been substantially discredited. Britain's great power status and extensive 'defence' commitments with its elaborate security/ intelligence networks have been areas of huge public interest and hence of confrontation. But the prosecution of individuals under the Official Secrets Act or its use to deny access to information has regularly left the government with egg on its face. The statement of the spy Kim Philby at a press conference in 1956 after being cleared by the prime minister of any taint of disloyalty was most ironic. Asked by a journalist if he could 'shed any light on the disappearance of Burgess and Maclean', Philby replied: 'No I can't . . . I am debarred by the Official Secrets Act from saying anything which might disclose to unauthorised persons information derived from my position as a former government official'.

In 1977, a year after the Franks Committee urged the replacement of the catch-all provisions of the Official Secrets Act, Duncan Campbell, then a journalist with *Time Out* was prosecuted with Crispin Aubrey and John Berry by a Labour government over an article which represented the first public admission of the existence of the communications interception organization, GCHQ – hardly a surprise to the Russians. Charges of 'collecting information' collapsed when Campbell was able to show that all the information he published was based on material available to the public. This included a reference to 'secret' microwave facilities which were actually marked on maps issued to Aeroflot pilots by the Civil Aviation Authority. Further charges were dismissed by the judge as 'oppressive'. This was not to be Duncan Campbell's last brush with the authorities who tried to suppress his documentary programme, *The Secret Society*, in 1984.

The prosecution of Sarah Tisdall for leaking details of the arrival date of Cruise missiles at Greenham Common – she was jailed for six months–contributed further to the discrediting of the Act to the point where a year later, a jury was prepared to defy all the evidence available, and the instructions of the judge, to acquit Clive Ponting. As a senior Ministry of Defence official he had leaked details of the British navy's attack on the Belgrano in 1982 to the MP Tam Dalyell, exposing the fact that the Commons had been misled on the issue.

When Cathy Massiter, an MI5 officer, went on to expose intelligence operations against trade unionists, civil liberties groups and leftwingers, the government knew that no jury would convict her and did not bother to prosecute.

The prosecution of the *Spycatcher* case was the final straw. While Peter Wright's book had been published all over the world, the government remorselessly pursued those who sought to publish in Britain. The case was eventually thrown out by the courts – a High Court judge told the governments that the absolute protection it was seeking could 'not be achieved this side of the Iron Curtain'.

The British government moved in 1989 to amend the Official Secrets Act, proclaiming the new Act as a move towards freedom of information, but in many respects it made matters worse. While reducing the number of categories of secrets, the government sought to make the disclosure of security and defence-related material an absolute offence to which a legal defence of public interest would not be possible. This even extends to the revelation of serious crime – and a journalist who hears such leaks may also face prosecution. 'In the armoury of criminal sanctions,' the lawyer Geoffrey Robertson writes, 'it replaces a blunderbuss with an Armalite rifle, trained on those who disclose precisely the kind of information which has caused public controversy and embarrassment in the past . . . Not a single document will be released as a result of its enactment.'[21]

More recently the Matrix Churchill affair has demonstrated only too clearly how little has changed in the attitude of British ministers to official secrets – and the essentially political character of their concerns. As the Scott inquiry is likely to demonstrate, ministers were prepared to see businessmen jailed rather than allow evidence to be placed before the courts that the accused had been acting with not only the full knowledge, but support of the government, in selling arms to Iraq. The revelations in no way jeopardized British defence or security, but were a devastating demonstration of political hypocrisy and double dealing.

In February 1992, in the midst of hostilities with Iraq, Civil Service Minister Tim Renton condemned a Freedom of Information Bill proposed by a Liberal Democrat MP. Writing in his local newspaper, Renton claimed the bill would mean the immediate publishing of cabinet minutes. 'It would mean that, for example, Saddam Hussein could apply to see the Cabinet Minutes on any Thursday afternoon, after a Cabinet meeting,' he thundered (while other members of his government were selling arms to the self-same Iraqi leader). Under the proposed bill, of course, these would have remained secret on the grounds of national security. Even the cabinet minister responsible for open government, William Waldegrave, told MPs that it is OK for ministers, on occasion, to lie to the Commons. There were also, he admitted, plenty of cases, when a minister will 'answer a question accurately . . . but he may not display everything he knows about the subject'.

When the British Freedom of Information Campaign was launched in 1984 its call for a Freedom of Information Act was firmly rejected by the then Prime Minister, Mrs Thatcher, as alien to the British system. 'Ministers' accountability to parliament would be reduced, and parliament itself diminished,' she claimed.

Yet the pressure did not go away, and in March 1994 the British Government issued new guidelines on official information, freeing new categories of government activity from the veil of secrecy. However, the new regulations do not give access to official documents, only to the information in them – as summarized by a civil servant. The suspicion will inevitably remain that the MP or member of the public will not get 'the whole truth' but a sanitized, politically safe version.

William Waldegrave's 'gaffe' is really a tacit acceptance of the need for a Right to Know Bill which would define precisely those areas in which a minister may legitimately refuse to answer questions, completely avoiding the necessity for being 'economical with the truth'.

THE SWEDISH MODEL – 'OFENTLIGHETSPRINCIPEN'

The Swedish experience reflects a fundamentally different approach to government and a political culture based on an entirely different relationship between governed and government. The tradition of open government goes back to the eighteenth century and the fifty years of what has become known as the Age of Liberty. With the death of Charles XII in 1718, Sweden's position as a great power and an absolute monarchy died too, and a remarkable democratic experiment started, the tradition of which still prevails.

In 1766 the Freedom of the Press Act was promulgated. It was largely the product of parliamentary rivalry and the realization by the government of the day that its turn in opposition would come – open government would allow some check on its rivals once they were in power. Its principal features remain in force today, despite intervening periods of absolute monarchy, and guarantee freedom of expression and, most remarkably for its time, access by citizens to almost all official documents – the principle of 'ofentlighetsprincipen'.

Importantly, the act is part of the fundamental law of the state, in essence the constitution, and can only be amended by two votes of the Riksdag (parliament) separated by a general election. The act's successor, the 1949 Freedom of the Press Act, was introduced because of concerns that during the Second World War important provisions had been circumvented.

Today the Swedish citizen can march into the prime minister's office any working day and demand to see the letters their leader has received that morning. The material must be produced promptly – tomorrow will not do – unless it falls under a narrow band of generally uncontentious exemptions. Access is free to all documents and no official is allowed to ask either the name of the person requesting the documentation or the purpose for which it is sought. Every government department, agency or local government office is obliged to set up a registry system in which details of correspondence and official documents are logged, and the head of the archives in the office is responsible for the classification and description of documents, and for public access.

The citizen has access to any 'official document' – draft documents are excepted – and so following the process of decision-making within and between ministries and government agencies is relatively straightforward for a diligent journalist. It is possible to examine anything from personnel files in local government, to the spending of your local school on food, to the foreign travel expenses claims of diplomats and politicians. All tenders for state work become public as soon as a contract is awarded, and the reports of inspectors on the environment, health or education are automatically available. A hospital patient or a social-welfare recipient has the right to full access to his/her files and all correspondence dealing with his/her case (except in special circumstances when a nominee acceptable to both sides has the access).

Olle Stenholm, the head of news in the Swedish Broadcasting Corporation, tells the story of a colleague who arrived early for an interview with the mayor of Malmo. Ushered into the mayor's empty office he sees a pile of post on the desk which he duly opens and reads. Not surprisingly, when the mayor arrives he is not a little unhappy to see the liberties being taken with his mail. The city lawyer is summoned but explains simply that the journalist is within his rights. 'The interview afterwards was distinctly frosty,' Stenholm admits.

The grounds for exceptions to the openness policy are very specifically set out in the fundamental law:

- The security of the state and relations with foreign governments and international organizations;
- Central finance policy, monetary policy, foreign exchange policy, or the public economic interest;
- Some of the inspection, control or other supervisory activities of a public authority;
- The interest of preventing or prosecuting crime;
- The protection of personal integrity or economic conditions of private citizens (although individual tax payments are public);
- The preservation of animal or plant species (important in cases like the nesting sites of rare birds).

To copperfasten the access to information Swedish civil servants are also constitutionally protected from either legal or disciplinary charges if they leak material that is exempted from the openness provisions (that right does not extend to personal information held by the state, or defence secrets). No leak inquiry is even permissible, although such leaks have to be for the purpose of publication – an indiscretion to a spouse over the breakfast table is not protected, as Lena Martusson, Professor of Administrative Law at Uppsala University, explains. There is no constitutional right to gossip, she says, but overall, legally 'the freedom to information is stronger than the duty of confidentiality'.

Journalists are similarly under an obligation to protect their sources and can be prosecuted if they fail to do so. The 'privilege' extends to testimony in court, although, in very exceptional circumstances a judge may overrule the protection where there is an overwhelming public interest at stake.

The rights under the Freedom of the Press Act are upheld by an independent parliamentary ombudsman, the Chancellor of Justice, in whom the sole right to prosecute is vested. Typically he is involved in considering a small number of cases every year – they usually vary from complaints that an official may not have reacted quickly enough to a request for documentation, to considering, as he did last year, whether to prosecute both a newspaper that revealed the source of a story and its source.

In the latter case a politician seeking to highlight funding cutbacks leaked details of individual cases in a social-welfare tribunal to a newspaper which revealed his name. The paper claimed it had a right to do so because the politician had only made a cursory attempt to protect the anonymity of the welfare clients. The politician demanded prosecution of the paper for revealing its source. In the end, with as much pragmatism as an eye for the law, the Chancellor let both off with a warning.

In an earlier case the Chancellor had considered a complaint from a member of the public who had sought documents from a defence-related agency. While the documents were not classified, the agency had refused to allow him into the building unless he gave his name for security clearance. Finally the agency had placed a table in the street outside the building at which he was allowed to read the requested documents. While he did so he was photographed by security staff. The Chancellor ruled that the agency had erred both in refusing access to the building – all state offices must now have a room where a citizen can inspect documents anonymously – and that it had no right to take his photograph.

The point that such cases make is that such rights – at present barely conceivable in Ireland – are taken, and protected, very seriously indeed. One Swedish minister lost her job recently, in part, for failing to register in the departmental archives correspondence with a party colleague who was making unofficial inquiries on her behalf into the death of Olaf Palme.

The system of 'ofenlightetsprincipen' is supported right across the political spectrum, and most vigorously – perhaps most surprisingly to Irish readers–by public servants themselves. The Swedish administrative structure is substantially different from that in Ireland. At the heart of government are small 'political' ministries which make policy, while day to day administration is carried out by very large government agencies whose civil servants pride themselves on their autonomy. It is a division of labour that works well and facilitates access to official information as the communications between agencies and ministries are all 'official' documents.

Civil servants deny that they are inhibited by the openness from offering contentious advice to ministers, and what they lose in terms of the supposed benefits of being able to give anonymous advice, they gain in protection from political interference by ministers in the work of government agencies. They also value the right to leak, an important check on abuse of authority.

The culture of openness has also created a degree of trust between public and state that has contributed to the cohesion of Swedish society and its political culture of consensus. Unlike Ireland there is little sense of an us and them attitude to the state. The *Dagens Nyheter* columnist, Inger Jagerhorn, argues that the reason is simply that 'the authorities in Sweden are considered to be the servants of the public . . . The State consists of the people'. It is a point made frequently by politicians of both right and left.

4. WILL IT WORK UNDER OUR SYSTEM?

In both Sweden and the United States, the approach to freedom of information is governed by the precepts of eighteenth-century rationalism. But under the Westminster system of government and jurisprudence, shared by most of Britain's former colonies, executive privilege is much greater. Governments, accountable only to parliament, have powers to ban or to make things secret, without having to worry about general legal principles such as those in the US Bill of Rights or the Swedish openness law. This is fertile ground for bureaucracy, for bans, proscriptions and secrecy.

Ireland has substantially adopted the Westminster system and the traditions of Whitehall live on. Under both the Official Secrets Act and the Offences Against the State Act, the powers of government ministers are quite remarkable.

It has been argued that the special relationship between the executive and administrative branches that is typical of the Westminster system is incompatible with freedom of information – that the machinery of government would collapse under the pressure of openness. Yet Canada, Australia and New Zealand are three examples of the Westminster system which have implemented freedom of information acts. Each of these countries passed the legislation in 1982, so that more than a decade of evidence on the effects of a freedom of information regime has piled up. And all of that evidence seems to show that they have been relatively successful. However, the Canadian example has some pitfalls which should not be reproduced in Irish legislation.

CANADA

The Canadian Access to Information Act (AIA) was accompanied in the same year, by a Privacy Act, governing the release of personal files. Each Act requires a Parliamentary Commissioner who acts as a sort of ombudsman. A complainant denied information may first appeal to the Information Commissioner for the release of material. The Commissioner may see secret government documents and can recommend but not compel disclosure.

Once the commissioner has ruled on a matter, the second, or judicial stage in the process can take place, so long as the information has not been disclosed. If the government department still refuses to release the information, despite the Commissioner's recommendation, the Commissioner can appeal to the federal courts to force disclosure. If the Commissioner has ruled against the complainant, s/he is also free to challenge that decision in the courts.

A majority (52 per cent) of cases have been resolved by the Information Commissioner without recourse to the courts.[22] Between 1983 and 1993, the first ten years of the Act, the Information Commissioner applied to the Federal Court on 49 occasions. In many of these cases, documents which had been delayed for many months were disclosed within two days. The workload for the Information and Privacy Commissioners in the twelve months up to March 1993 amounted to 720 information complaint investigations and 477 privacy complaints. This is for a population of 26.5 million. Roughly scaled down to fit the Irish population, these figures would read 95 and 65 respectively, or around 160 complaints a year if both functions came under one office. Of course, the first years of operation would see much higher complaints figures as the effects of the law began to filter through. Canada's Information Commissioner has a staff of 32 and a budget of $1.8m.[23] Cases where departments refused to disclose information took an average of 5.58 months to complete, but some complaints took much less time.

Although the AIA represents a major improvement on the pre-1982 situation, it has not eliminated government secrecy or bureaucratic foot-dragging. A Campaign for Open Government was set up in the summer of 1993. Exorbitant government charges for releasing information are among the campaign's central targets. Peter Calami, one of its founders, compares the cost of certain geographical data from the US Bureau of Statistics with that of its Canadian equivalent. In the US, a computer disk containing 450 megabytes of information cost $99 while Statistics Canada charged $450,000 for comparable data.[24] The Campaign for Open Government argues that far more material could be downloaded electronically for the users of infonets at virtually no cost to the state. It also calls on government agencies not to use copyright as an excuse for not releasing documents or data.[25]

AUSTRALIA AND NEW ZEALAND

Under the Australian Freedom of Information Act (FIA), complainants must first appeal to the body refusing the information to allow a review of the decision. The process of internal review entails a re-examination of the decision by a more senior member of the relevant department. If the department still refuses to divulge the information, the complainant may either appeal to the Commonwealth and Defence Forces Ombudsman or to the Administrative Appeals Tribunal.

The Ombudsman, like the Canadian Commissioner, has only the power to recommend, not to order disclosure. This office is less likely than its Canadian counterpart to challenge government departments. S/he will not recommend that a decision is altered, if it is one of a number of 'reasonable' courses of action that could have been taken. Complaining to the Ombudsman avoids legal costs and is preferred in cases where no major legal questions are involved. The Administrative Appeals Tribunal's proceedings are public and are adversarial, as in a normal court of law, with the right to cross-question witnesses, etc. The decision of the Tribunal is binding.

The internal review process results in the disclosure of a considerable amount of information, for the small percentage of people who avail of it, but only 4.2 per cent of those who had been refused information sought internal review in the year 1991–1992. Full access was granted to roughly 10 per cent of these. In 60 per cent of appeals, the original refusal was upheld and 30 per cent were given part of the information they sought. In the same year, there were 45 appeals to the Administrative Appeals Tribunal and 76 complaints to the Ombudsman. Two further cases went to other courts.[26]

Over 28,000 requests for information were made under the Freedom of Information Act in the year 1991–1992. Of these, 76 per cent were granted in full, 19 per cent granted in part, and 4 per cent were refused. The Australian Act sets a thirty-day limit on information requests, and 71 per cent of requests were dealt with in this period. The annual cost for 1991–1992 was $6m.

In New Zealand, the Official Information Act is enforced by an Ombudsman. Here the Ombudsman's decisions on disclosure are binding, unless vetoed by a government Order in Council within twenty-one days. Sir George Laking, a former New Zealand Ombudsman, distinguishes his function from that of the ordinary ombudsman thus:

> I am not, as under the Ombudsmen Act, deciding whether a departmental decision or action is unjust, unreasonable discriminatory or wrong. I am called on to decide, much as a Court would do, whether the department or organisation has, first, interpreted correctly the provisions of the Act and, secondly, provide an adequate justification of its decision to withhold information.[27]

FEARS EXAGGERATED

Mr Justice Michael Kirby, President of the New South Wales Court of Appeal, reports scathingly on the fears expressed in advance of the Freedom of Information Act: 'Various extravagant claims were made, namely that this act would result in: the fall of the Westminster system of government as we had known it; the loss of frankness and candour amongst public servants; the inability of the government to function properly when its every action was open to public scrutiny; and the imposition of inordinate costs and the ultimate triumph of lawyerly concern with the process rather than the outcome of administrative action . . . None of these dire prognostications has been borne out.'[28]

Before the legislation, government departments were asked to estimate how many information requests they expected to receive. The disparity between their predictions and the reality bears out Judge Kirby's point:

Department	Expected annual requests	Actual requests (1985–86)
Attorney General	3,000–5,000	313
Health	16,000	334
Immigration and Ethnic Affairs	100,000	1,582
Primary Industry	12,500	54
Prime Minister and Cabinet	1,000	89
Treasury	600	54
Trade Practice Commission	2,000	18

In fact, most Australian agencies receive very few requests for information. Less than 40 complaints were received by 72 per cent of departments in 1991–1992, and 54 per cent received less than 10 requests. The vast majority (93 per cent) of all requests went to the departments of Veteran's Affairs, Social Security, Immigration and Ethnic Affairs and the Taxation Office. These are the agencies which have the largest numbers of personal files.[29]

John Grace, Canadian Information Commissioner, tells a similar story:

Embarking on a freedom of information regime is, for many, akin to stepping off a precipice into the darkness. You'll find, I can assure you, that it's no more than a six-inch drop. Bureaucrats' and politicians' lives will change only on the margin. They certainly won't die from the impact![30]

A commonly-expressed objection to freedom of information legislation is that it may damage the relationship between government ministers and their civil servants. The New Zealand Information Authority reported in 1986 that, before the Official Information Act,

> it was felt by some that it could bring about a change in the relationships between ministers and the permanent heads [of government departments]; that the possibility of conflict could arise if it was seen that there was a divergence of views between the department and the minister. In the perceptions of permanent heads, this has not eventuated and they do not see any substantive changes in their relationships with the ministers.[31]

In 1991, Robert Hazell studied the effects of freedom of information legislation in Canada, New Zealand and Australia. He noted the fears that advice 'would no longer be put in writing, or that it would be heavily diluted' and searched hard for evidence of this phenomenon. While he recognized that fears still remained in certain quarters, he was unable to come up with any actual evidence.

> Of the two permanent secretaries I interviewed in Australia, both said that they had noticed no reduction in the frankness of official advice which flowed across their desk on its way up to the minister. One of them had certainly feared this would happen; but his fears had not been borne out in practice.[32]

Judge Kirby provides additional corroboration: 'Ministerial responsibility has been found to be entirely compatible with freedom of information legislation in Australia, Canada [and] New Zealand.' Openness seems to have instead refined the standards of bureaucratic English. The Legal and Constitutional Committee of the Parliament of Victoria (Australia) reported in 1989: 'Written communications appear to have improved. For example, the Health Department reports which once resembled streams of consciousness have now become succinct and to the point.'[33]

Hazell would agree. In a 1989 study of Commonwealth openness legislation he wrote that 'access to personal files has been a success story'. Whether 'in prisons, in personnel, tax or social security, it is generally acknowledged that there has been an improvement in the quality of reports about agency clients. There is now a fairer assessment of individuals, with less unsubstantiated and prejudicial comment . . .'[34] The Australian Attorney General told a similar story in 1985, detailing the improvements in various departments due to freedom of information. In Social Security, 'mistrust and dissatisfaction' had been lessened by making details available to clients and the number of appeals against decisions had been reduced. In Industry and Commerce, bad decisions had been reversed and in the Department of the Territories and Local Government, procedures had been streamlined and made more consistent.[35] Even the Royal Canadian Mounted Police seems to be happy that freedom of information won't stop them getting their man. The Canadian Privacy Commissioner reported in 1986 that neither the police nor anyone else had complained that the right of individuals to see their personal records was 'causing valuable sources of information to dry up'. Sensitive information seems to have been protected. Elsewhere in the report, the Commissioner emphasizes that openness has not deterred officers from making full reports on individuals: 'The primeval human urge to record information seems to overcome any apprehensions of danger or embarrassment from the Privacy Act.'[36]

The point was repeated seven years later by the present Information Commissioner, John Grace: 'Won't public servants fear the free flow of information and stop writing things down? No, that has simply not happened. . . . Not writing things down is simply not a practical option, no matter how cautious a bureaucrat wishes to be. Public servants have an irresistible compulsion to create files.'[37]

In 1979, as the Australian Freedom of Information Act was being mooted, the Senate Standing Committee on Constitutional Affairs issued the following statement:

> 'We value the Westminster system of government; we do not seek to change it; nor do we believe effective freedom of information legislation would change it . . . Very often people have alleged that the Westminster system is under attack by freedom of information legislation when what is actually under attack is their own traditional and convenient way of doing things, immune from public gaze and scrutiny. We are indeed seeking to put an end to that. What matters is not the convenience of ministers or public servants, but what contributes to better government.'[38]

This emphasis has drawn an echo even from the highest reaches of Whitehall. Sir Douglas Wass, former Permanent Secretary to the Treasury and Joint Head of the Home Civil Service has said:

> With its current insistence on 'good governance' for others, now is perhaps an opportune moment for the British government to show an example by embracing freedom of information as a democratic right.

HEAVY COSTS OF SECRECY

Under the Westminster system, as we have already discussed in relation to the Dáil, new information is mainly divulged through parliamentary questions. But there are many ways in which ministers can evade this responsibility. The Canadian Information Commissioner, John Grace, makes the point that a freedom of information regime will enhance the powers of members of parliament, not bypass them:

> Access to information rights are at least as important to a member of parliament as they are to an ordinary citizen . . . the Access to Information Act can return power to Parliament . . . The chances are . . . that a request made under the access Act will yield better results than a written question placed on the Order Paper. Written questions produce, if anything, the briefest of answers, not documents . . . [members of parliament], by using the Access to Information Act routinely and frequently, can force government to share information and reclaim a historic right.

To avoid the truth, it's not even necessary to go as far as William Waldegrave did in defending parliamentary statements that amount to creative accounting. All ministers have to do is to refuse to answer difficult questions on the grounds of cost. It is quite in order for a minister to claim that the research costs of answering a particular question are disproportionate to the gain from the information. In October 1987, Labour MP, Tony Banks asked the British Prime Minister to state what 'disproportionate cost' meant in real cash terms. Mrs Thatcher replied that, if answering a question would cost more than £200, it would be up to the relevant minister to decide whether the cost was too high. Banks then asked Thatcher how many questions she had refused to answer since 1979 on the grounds of disproportionate costs: 'This information can be supplied only at disproportionate cost,' came the reply.[39]

Opponents of openness often make similar claims that it is too costly. In fact the opposite is the case. Freedom of information saves money as well as lives. Disclosures under the Australian Act in 1986 led to the cancellation of a AUS$270m project, every penny of which would have been wasted if it had gone ahead. The Australian Army was seeking to buy a 2.5 million hectare site in New South Wales for use as a tank training ground. Local protesters secured documents which proved that the site was fog-bound for most of the year and that it was far too mountainous for the purpose. As the Australian Army normally has to function in tropical conditions, training in an alpine climate was deemed rather inappropriate and a better site was selected.[40]

In Canada, openness legislation exposed the fact that a Can$1bn (£500 m) subsidy to grain farmers in 1987 was unnecessary. It was designed to compensate farmers for low prices caused by a trade war. The farmers however, were already subsidised under another programme. This unnecessary grant was promised two weeks before a provincial election. The Access to Information Act also allowed the publication of documents which showed that four of Canada's nuclear reactors had been allowed to function for eight years with what nuclear regulators called 'inadequate' safety systems.

'In terms of the total cost of administration, the marginal cost of freedom of information is relatively slight,' said Judge Kirby in 1993. 'Even if, in part, freedom of information encourages more attention to honesty, lawfulness, integrity and better decision-making for fear of subsequent disclosure, that will be no bad thing.'

Michael Duffy, Australian Attorney General, agrees: 'The total cost to the Commonwealth [of Australia] is minimal in comparison to the benefit to the community. Generally, agencies have accepted that the Freedom of Information Act has a place within their normal functions and make allowances in staffing and administrative budgets to cover the cost of the legislation.'

Canadian Commissioner John Grace points out that the greater the openness, the lower the cost of implementing it: 'Costs also depend upon efficiency and how open the institution is; openness means fewer formal requests, less time taken with complaints.'

5. Letting in the Light?

When he succeeded Charles Haughey to the leadership of Fianna
Fáil, Albert Reynolds' declared intention was to 'let in the light' on
Irish society. And, to a great extent, the election of November 1992
was about letting in the light. The government which emerged was
a novelty not only in bringing together a new-look Fianna Fáil and
an invigorated, massively expanded Labour Party, but also in the
extent to which the government pledged itself to potentially far-
reaching changes in a largely discredited political system.

The Programme for a Partnership Government, in a chapter entitled
'Broadening of Democracy', promised, 'in line with our commitment to open government and transparency', an ethics in government bill; a new register of interests for politicians, senior civil
servants and managers of state firms; registration of gifts to office-
holders and of significant donations to political parties; state
funding for parties and curbs on spending by candidates. The
Oireachtas would be reformed, upgrading the committee system
and easing the *sub judice* rule. Individual TDs would get the right to
introduce non-controversial legislation, MEPs would be integrated
into the work of the Oireachtas, local government would be
reformed. And, the programme promised, 'We will consider the
introduction of freedom of information legislation.' Indeed, the
'Minister for Ethics', Eithne Fitzgerald, has been involved in
considerable preparatory work on just such legislation which, she
says, will be 'the priority of my department' as soon as the Ethics
in Government Bill is out of the way. But although the minister is
well disposed to freedom of information, Fianna Fáil's programme
negotiators were hostile to any hard commitment.

The legislation being framed by Eithne Fitzgerald, reflects
much of the international experience. Her priority, she says, is
with individual citizens' access to information held on them by the
state, their ability to ensure it is correct, and to the transparency

of the state's dealings with them. She cites, for example, the need to publish guidelines for dealing with social welfare recipients and means-testing regulations and says that work is already being done to make such documents accessible.

On the more general issue of public access to the workings of government, the proposed legislation starts with a presumption of openness and transparency, replacing the blanket bans of the Official Secrets Act with specific and largely uncontroversial exemptions. Those exemptions fall into seven broad categories:

- National security and relations with foreign countries;
- Private personal details or details of third parties;
- Details of police or state agency investigations that may lead to criminal prosecution, and of state legal arguments;
- Sensitive national budget information or details of state contracts or the tendering process;
- Commercial secrets of value to competitors of state firms;
- Information given in secrecy;
- Advice given before a policy decision is taken.

The framing of the latter exemption will provide one of the key tests by which the commitment to open government will be judged. The exemption has the potential to undermine substantially the intent of the legislation.

The minister argues that it is important not to contaminate the policy process – 'People should be able to toss things around without fear,' she argues, as decision-making is often best done 'by considering the way-out and the outrageous among a range of options'. The danger is that civil servants who fear that their memos will be published may not proffer the best advice, only the most politically acceptable.

In fact, as we record elsewhere, the evidence is that the quality of advice to ministers does not necessarily suffer from public scrutiny. In its draft Freedom of Information Bill the British Campaign for Freedom of Information addresses the issue by distinguishing between 'objective' and 'subjective' policy advice, arguing that any such exemption should not apply to factual information or its analysis, interpretation or evaluation; to projections based on factual information; or to expert advice. Nor is there any reason why, when documents incorporate both types of advice, they should not be released in an edited form.

The other exemption to openness provisions which is of particular concern is the restriction on material relating to relations with foreign countries. In Sweden the issue has become the focus of an important debate on EU accession: documents previously available under the Freedom of the Press Act, it is feared, will be lost under a veil of secrecy because the competence of the Union extends to areas previously regarded as solely domestic.

At the time of going to press the Swedes propose to ease the problem by amending the law to allow classification of foreign relations material to be optional instead of mandatory. Then the issue becomes one of the culture of the public service and the willingness of individual public servants to assist in creating a climate of openness – largely not a problem in Sweden, but of importance in countries where a new tradition is being created.

Experience in Ireland of attitudes to answering parliamentary questions and of the response to the recent EU environmental information directive suggests, however, that a public service tradition of minimalist disclosure will not change without the legal enshrining of specific new rights and responsibilites. Both New Zealand and Australia enshrine in their freedom of information legislation a positive duty on public servants to assist people who are looking for information, to help them in preparing applications and to steer them in the direction of sources they may not be aware of. Legislation should also make it clear that in grey areas, the duty of the public servant responsible for classification of documents shall be to lean in the direction of disclosure. Those applying for information should be fully informed both of their rights and of the detailed reasons for any refusal.

The minister has also, importantly, indicated a willingness to incorporate provisions to protect whistle-blowing civil servants. This would allow a public servant to expose wrongdoing in government by offering a defence (to allegations of leaking genuinely classified material) of an overwhelming public interest. The 'overwhelming public interest' argument should also be a ground for appeal to the commissioner in respect of documents denied to an ordinary member of the public.

Specific provision also needs to be made to ensure that the response to requests for information is speedy. Although the Swedes insist on an immediate response, a thirty-day time-scale is more typical internationally. This allows for the reference of sensitive material to an ombudsman and for affected third parties to respond.

Eithne Fitzgerald's proposals provide for the right of appeal by the public to an independent freedom of information commissioner similar to the Data Protection Commissioner, and a right of further appeal by both the public and authorities to the courts. It is important, however, to minimize the costly and lengthy use of the courts by ensuring that such a commissioner be given more than an advisory role – he or she should have the power to order the release of documents and, where necessary, their correction.

Two other key issues yet to be resolved are the question of charges and of the scope of the proposed legislation. The minister appears committed to ensuring that all access by individuals to their personal files will be free, but talks ominously of the need for some charges for the more general access to state documents. If such charges are only aimed at recovering the cost of photocopying, then there can be no objection in principle. What is at stake here, however, is an attempt to establish a new democratic right, but essentially a right of the same type as the right to vote. In principle there should be no charges for access to the workings of democracy.

On a more practical level, charges would inhibit the use of the system by those most in need of access to public documents –

community and public-interest groups whose research is largely carried out by volunteers and whose resources are invariably scarce. Students, academics, and free-lance journalists would also be seriously hampered. Concerns that an absence of charges may lead to 'abuse' of the system by journalists on what might be called 'trawling expeditions' – unspecific and time-consuming searches of huge quantities of documents in the hope of something turning up – can be met by giving the ombudsman limited powers to curtail what he or she regards as vague and unreasonable requests.

The scope of the legislation is also critical, both in terms of the records and organizations covered. Records need to be defined as including those held on paper, computer, film, tape or other form. Once again the model proposed by the British Campaign for Freedom of Information sets a useful definition of 'public authorities':

> government departments, nationalised industries, health authorities, executive bodies such as the Health and Safety Executive and the National Rivers Authority, agencies such as the Driver and Vehicle Licensing Agency, a large number of advisory bodies such as the Committee on the Safety of Medicines and the Advisory Committee on Women's Employment, and other bodies which receive at least half their funds from central government or to whom ministers appoint one or more members.

Although we have fewer quangos in Ireland than in Britain, the list should range from the records of such bodies as the Department of the Environment to Dublin Corporation and the Eastern Health Board. It should encompass, subject to the exemptions mentioned, organizations as diverse as Bord Fáilte, the Abbey Theatre, FÁS, the Blood Transfusion Service, the National Rehabilitation Board,

Aer Lingus and Iarnród Éireann, a local national school as much as University College, Galway, the Labour Relations Commission, the National Museum, the Agency for Personal Service Overseas, the District Court Offices, the OPW Building Maintenance Workshop, the Censorship of Publications Board . . . and the Office of the Freedom of Information Commissioner.

All such organizations should be under an obligation to appoint an official responsible for processing requests for information and for maintaining a comprehensive public register of documents. Larger organizations should be obliged to make provision for facilities for the public to inspect records.

A LEAP OF FAITH

What is required above all, however, is a leap of faith by our government. Along with action on the promises of open government and transparency, we need a new sense from our political establishment that the citizens of this state can be trusted, that they are mature enough to take the right decisions for themselves, that they no longer need the protective mollycoddling of one of the most paternalistic states in Europe.

We can take heart from the sophistication of the electorate in its complex judgement on the abortion referendums. And the government, in lifting the order under Section 31 of the Broadcasting Act, has itself paid tribute to the maturity and commitment to democratic values of the people.

In a sense, the late 1980s has seen Irish democracy at last crossing something akin to the alcoholic's psychological barrier of denial. We no longer pretend there are no problems by refusing to talk about them openly. We can now begin to confront problems head on. The demand for freedom of information is not a call for a new abstract right, but a practical way of facing up to those problems – most specifically to the alienation of citizens from a state that they regard with increasing distrust. Ireland is not Italy or Japan, but we too have our golden circles.

True democracies are in the end far more robust than tyrannies – and than paternalistic democracies—precisely because democracies rest on the active, conscious participation of the citizen, on a consent that is stronger, more genuine, and more freely given because it is informed.

Arguing in around 430 BC for popular participation in ancient Athens, Pericles succinctly summed up the case against elitism: 'Although,' he said, 'only a few may originate a policy, we are all able to judge it.' It seems we have yet to learn the lesson.

NOTES AND REFERENCES

Much of the material in this pamphlet is drawn from the excellent work of the British Campaign for Freedom of Information, specifically from that of Maurice Frankel, and from Geoffrey Robertson's *Freedom, the Individual and the Law*. Thanks are also due to Brian Trench, Tony Heffernan and the Minister of State at the Department of the Tánaiste, Eithne Fitzgerald.

1. The relevant British Acts date from 1911 and 1920.

2. See *Dáil Debates* for 27, 28 March and 5 April 1962.

3. Official Secrets Act 1963, Sec 4 (1).

4. *Dáil Debates*, 5 April 1962. Haughey added that 'Effluxion of time makes any document unsecret, if you like, but the fact that the document was marked secret puts everybody on his guard not to disclose the contents.'

5. A full account of the proceedings can be found in *Irish Law Reports Monthly '93*, Vol. 13, No. 2, pp. 81–128.

6. *Beef Tribunal Proceedings*, 15 Jan 1992, p. 60.

7. This fact was recognized by Minister of State Noel Dempsey; see *Dáil Debates*, 4 May 1993, pp. 354–68.

8. Letter from the Office of the Ceann Comhairle to De Rossa, dated 28 March 1994 (Ref: D15/11).

9. Letter from the Office of the Ceann Comhairle to De Rossa, dated 28 May 1993 (Ref: A1 R1).

10. Letter from the Office of the Ceann Comhairle to De Rossa, dated 6 October 1993 (Ref: A1 D15/).

11. Letter from the Office of the Ceann Comhairle to Pat O'Malley TD, dated 23 May 1989 (Ref: D15/17).

12. Written answer to Dáil Question No. 61, Wednesday 24 May 1989.

13. 'Government and Dáil', Basil Chubb in *De Valera's Constitution and Ours*, Brian Farrell (ed.), Dublin 1988, p. 99.

14. 'Politics and Change', Brian Farrell in *Ireland in Transition*, Kieran A. Kennedy (ed.), Cork 1986, pp. 146–47.

15. The New York Times *v* The United States, 403 US 713 (1971) at 729.

16. The European Court of Human Rights, 1976: Handyside judgement.

17. *Council of Europe Activities in the Media Field*, Directorate of Human Rights, Strasburg 1993.

18. The European Court of Human Rights, 1990: Autonic AG judgement.

19. The European Court of Human Rights, 1986: Lingens judgement.

20. *Access to Information on the Environment*, Department of the Environment, Dublin 1993.

21. *Freedom, the Individual and the Law*, Geoffrey Robertson, Harmondsworth 1991.

22. The information detailed here and below is from the Information Commissioner of Canada's *Annual Report* 1992–1993.

23. The Canadian government estimates the cost of the Access to Information Act at $12m per annum, but it is important to note that the current Information Commissioner, John Grace, disputes this figure. In February 1993, he told a London conference 'Overall costs attributable to the . . . Act are enormously and notoriously difficult to quantify. All such costs should be taken with the proverbial grain of salt. Governments have vested interests in exaggerating costs.'

24. 'The Emerging Information Underclass', Peter Calami, *Media* magazine.

25. The Canadian Campaign for Open Government can be contacted at PO Box 828, Station B, Ottawa, Ontario, K1P 5P9.

26. Australian Government Freedom of Information Act 1982, *Annual Report* 1991–1992.

27. Quoted in M. Taggart, 'Courts, Ombudsmen and Freedom of Information: The Empire Strikes Back' *Victoria University of Wellington Law Review*, 1990, 20, Monograph 2.

28. Address to conference of the British Campaign for Freedom of Information, London, February 1993.

29. *Annual Report* by the Attorney General on the Operation of the Freedom of Information Act 1991–1992.

30. Address to conference of the British Campaign for Freedom of Information, London, February 1993.

31. Report quoted in *Secrets* No. 23, November 1991, a publication of the British Campaign for Freedom of Information.

32. 'Freedom of Information: Lessons from Canada, Australia and New Zealand', R. Hazell in *Policy Studies*, Autumn 1991.

33. Report quoted in *Secrets* No. 23, November 1991.

34. R. Hazell 'Freedom of Information in Australia, Canada and New Zealand' in *Public Administration*, Summer 1989.

35. Australian Attorney General's report 1983–1984.

36. Canadian Privacy Commissioner, *Annual Report*, 1984–1985.

37. Address to conference of the British Campaign for Freedom of Information, London, February 1993.

38. Quoted in *Secrets*, No. 23, November 1991.

39. Hansard, 29 October 29 1987.

40. Maurice Frankel, 'Why Britain Needs a Freedom of Information Act' in *London Public Policy Review*, Spring 1993.

APPENDIX 1

Council of Europe Ministerial Declaration, 29 April 1982:

The member States of the Council of Europe:

1 Considering that the principles of genuine democracy, the rule of law and respect for human rights form the basis of their co-operation, and that freedom of expression and information is a fundamental element of those principles;

2 Considering that this freedom has been proclaimed in national constitutions and international instruments, and in particular in Article 19 of the Universal Declaration of Human Rights and in Article 10 of the European Convention on Human Rights; . . .

4 Considering that the freedom of expression and information is necessary for the social, economic, cultural development of every human being, and constitutes a condition for the harmonious progress of social and cultural groups, nations and the international community; . . .

6 Convinced that states have the duty to guard against infringements of the freedom of expression and information and should adopt policies designed to foster as much as possible a variety of media and a plurality of information sources, thereby allowing a plurality of ideas and opinions; . . .

    i Reaffirm their firm attachment to the principles of freedom of expression and information as a basic element of democratic and pluralist society;

    ii Declare that in the field of freedom of information and mass media they seek to achieve the following objectives: a) protection of the right of everyone, regardless of frontiers, to express himself, to seek and receive information and ideas, whatever their source, as well as to impart them under the conditions set out in Article 10 of the European Convention on Human Rights; b) absence of censorship or any arbitrary controls or constraints on participants in the information process, or media content or on the transmission and dissemination of information; c) the pursuit of an open information policy in the public sector, including access to information, in order to enhance the individual's understanding of, and his ability to discuss freely political, social, economic and cultural matters; . . .

iii Resolve to intensify their co-operation in order: a) to defend the right of everyone to the exercise of freedom of expression and information; b) to promote, through teaching and education, the effective exercise of the freedom of expression and information; c) to promote the free flow of information, thus contributing to international understanding, a better knowledge of convictions and traditions, respect for the diversity of opinions and the mutual enrichment of cultures; d) to share their experience and knowledge in the media field; e) to ensure that new information and communication techniques and services, where available, are effectively used to broaden the scope of freedom of expression and information.

The declaration – effectively a commitment by all the member states, including Ireland, to enact freedom of information legislation – came a year after the Council of Ministers' recommendation R(81)19, to member states on the access to information held by public authorities. It is, in effect, the outline of what such legislation should contain:

i Everyone within the jurisdiction of a member state shall have the right to obtain on request, information held by the public authorities other than legislative bodies and judicial authorities.

ii Effective and adequate means shall be provided to provide access to information.

iii Access to information shall not be refused on the ground that the requesting person has not a specific interest in the matter.

iv Access to information shall be provided on the basis of equality.

v The foregoing principles shall apply subject only to such limitations and restrictions as are necessary in a democratic society for the the protection of legitimate public interests (such as national security, public safety, public order, the economic well-being of the country, the prevention of crime, or for preventing the disclosure of information received in confidence), and for the protection of privacy and other legitimate private interests, having, however, due regard to the specific interest of an individual in information held by the public authorities which concerns him personally.

vi Any request for information shall be decided upon within a reasonable time.

vii A public authority refusing access to information shall give the reasons on which the refusal is based, according to law or practice.

viii Any refusal of information shall be subject to review on request.

APPENDIX 2

Article 10 of the European Declaration of Human Rights (1950):

1. Everyone has the right to freedom of expression. This right shall include freedom to hold opinions and to receive and impart information and ideas without interference by public authority and regardless of frontiers. This article shall not prevent states from requiring the licensing of broadcasting, television or cinema enterprises.

2. The exercise of these freedoms, since it carries with it duties and responsibilities, may be subject to such formalities, conditions, restrictions or penalties as are prescribed by law and are necessary in a democratic society, in the interests of national security, territorial integrity or public safety, for the prevention of disorder or crime, for the protection of health or morals, for the protection of the reputation or rights of others, for preventing the disclosure of information received in confidence, or for maintaining the authority and impartiality of the judiciary.

APPENDIX 3

Article 19 of the Universal Declaration of Human Rights (1948):

Everyone has the right to freedom of opinion and expression; this right includes freedom to hold opinions without interference and to seek, receive and impart information and ideas through any media and regardless of frontiers.

APPENDIX 4

Patrick Smyth and Ronan Brady are founder-members of 'Let in the Light', a non-partisan campaign against censorship and secrecy. It was established in January 1993 following a hugely successful conference in Dublin addressed by among others, Salman Rushdie, Carl Bernstein, Anthony Lewis, Kevin Boyle, Anthony Clare, Garret Fitzgerald, representatives of Article 19, the International Federation of Journalists, the National Union of Journalists and SIPTU (sponsorship from both of the latter organizations is gratefully acknowledged). The proceedings were published as *Let in the Light* (Brandon, 1993).

'Let in the Light' can be contacted: c/o Ronan Brady, 33 Geraldine St, Dublin 7.